CHET ATKINS C.G.P. *almost alone*

CONTENTS

Music transcriptions by John Knowles, with Christian Denoyelle, Byron Fogo, and Bill Piburn.

ISBN 0-7935-6875-7

7777 W. Bluemound Rd. P.O. Box 13819 Milwaukee, WI 53213

a note from Chet Atkins

I was almost alone when I recorded the tunes on this album. I say "almost" because I invited several musicians I admire to join me on individual cuts. Randy Goodrum played keyboards on "I Still Write Your Name in the Snow," Randy Howard played fiddle on "Sweet Alla Lee," and Paul Yandell played acoustic guitar on "Maybelle." Bergen White did the string arrangements and the Nashville String Machine performed them.

When I recorded "I Still Write Your Name in the Snow," I replaced the fifth and sixth strings on a Country Gentleman guitar with electric bass strings to get that full sound. With the exception of "You Do Something to Me" and "Jam Man," there are no guitar overdubs. It is just me and my big foot. On "You Do Something to Me," I overdubbed a resonator guitar about midway through the tune. "Jam Man" utilizes a musical tool by that name which makes it possible to lay down a rhythm track and then layer other parts. I sometimes feature it in my shows, with the guitar doing all the music parts and my right hand overdubbing percussion sounds. A Les Paul I'm not! But it's fun to try.

I know that John Knowles, Christian Denoyelle, Byron Fogo, and Bill Piburn spent a lot of time alone with the album, transcribing the tunes. Now it's your turn to spend a lot of time alone with the book, the album, and your guitar.

Have fun!

Chet Atkins, C. G. P.

tips on playing Chet's music

by John Knowles

Chet plays with a thumbpick and three fingers. You can play most of these tunes without a thumbpick and still get a good result, but you won't get Chet's tone and rhythmic drive. Some of Chet's moves can be adapted to a "flat-pick-and-two-fingers" technique, but overall, you'll get the best results playing fingerstyle all the way.

The right-hand fingering is shown by the letters *p*, *i*, *m*, and *a,* where *p* stands for thumb, *i* for index, *m* for middle, and *a* for ring.

In "Jam Man" (page 19, section B), Chet's thumb plays the stem-down notes to produce an alternating-bass accompaniment. The stem-up melody-notes are played with *i, m,* and an occasional *a*. Because these 16 bars recur throughout the tune, you can play along with Chet's recording to perfect your timing and feel.

Chet uses a similar alternating-bass pattern in "Big Foot," "Happy Again," "Sweet Alla Lee," "Maybelle," "Cheek to Cheek," and "I Still Write Your Name in the Snow" (page 31, Guitar Solo). He varies the alternating-bass pattern in "You Do Something to Me" and "Mr. Bojangles."

In "A Little Mark Music" (page 11, section A), Chet begins with a right-hand pattern where thumb and index sound notes on the same string. Then he uses a variation on the alternating-bass pattern for two bars (page 11, section B). These two patterns recur throughout the tune.

Chet uses several right-hand patterns to create turnarounds, embellish melodies, and play scales. In "A Little Mark Music" (page 15, section E, measure 15), he plays a turnaround based on an *m-i-p* pattern. He uses a similar pattern, *p-m-i,* to embellish the melody to "Mr. Bojangles" (page 63, section J). That three-finger roll makes 3/4 time sound like 6/8 time.

Chet uses an unusual *i-p-i-m* roll to embellish the melody in "Cheek to Cheek" (page 70, section I). The first sixteenth note of each group of four is played on the first string to bring out the melody.

He gets a different effect with the *i-p-i-m* pattern in "Jam Man" (page 26, section I). This time, the first eighth note of each group of four is played on the second string. He uses the same right-hand pattern in the harmony part.

In "Big Foot" (page 6, section H), Chet plays a two-octave scale using a *p-m-i* pattern. He begins the scale with his *i* finger so he is always crossing to the next higher string with *m.* There is a similar scale at the beginning of "You Do Something to Me" (page 71, section A).

When Chet plays a descending scale, as in "Jam Man" (page 25, section H, measure 13), he uses the same *p-m-i* pattern, but he crosses to the next lower string with *p*.

Chet has some unusual techniques for incorporating harmonics into his playing. Both natural and artificial harmonics are notated at actual pitch by a diamond-shaped note-head on the staff. Natural harmonics are labeled "Harm" while artificial harmonics are labeled "A. H."

The natural harmonics are notated by TAB numbers in brackets <> for the fret at which Chet touches the string with a left-hand finger to produce the harmonic. For example, see "Ave Maria" (page 79. section F, measure 6).

Artificial harmonics are notated by TAB numbers in brackets <> that show the fret at which Chet presses the string. He touches the string twelve frets above the TAB number with the tip of his right index-finger and sounds the harmonic with his thumbpick. For example, see "Jam Man" (page 20, section D).

Chet also plays a lick that combines artificial harmonics with regular notes and pull-offs to produce a scale effect. It almost sounds like all of the notes are harmonics. He uses this lick in "Jam Man" (page 21, measure 1).

As much as we have tried to convey how to play these tunes like Chet, you'll get closer by listening to and playing along with Chet's recorded performances. All of the tunes in this book are from Chet's album *Almost Alone* (Columbia CK-67497) which is available on CD or cassette. It's easier to find a particular song or passage on a CD.

If you would like to find out more about Chet's style of playing, write to The Chet Atkins Appreciation Society, c/o Mark Pritcher, 3716 Timberlake Road, Knoxville, TN 37920, or to me, c/o John Knowles' FingerStyle Quarterly, P. O. Box 120355, Nashville, TN 37212.

Big Foot

Written by Chet Atkins

A
E7
1/2 1/4
A
D7
A6
E7
A
E
D6
E13
A
D7
A
D6
F°7
F♯m
B7
E+7

F
A
D
A9
G
D7
A7
E7
1/4
E9
A13
D7
A
F9
E9
A
H
N.C.
i p m i p
I
D7
A
A7
E7

A
D7
A
F9
E9
A
J
N.C.
K
D9
A
E7
A
D7
A
E7
Free Time
(foot)
A9
let ring

Waiting for Susie B.

Written by Chet Atkins

Tuning:
① = E ④ = D
② = B ⑤ = G
③ = G ⑥ = C

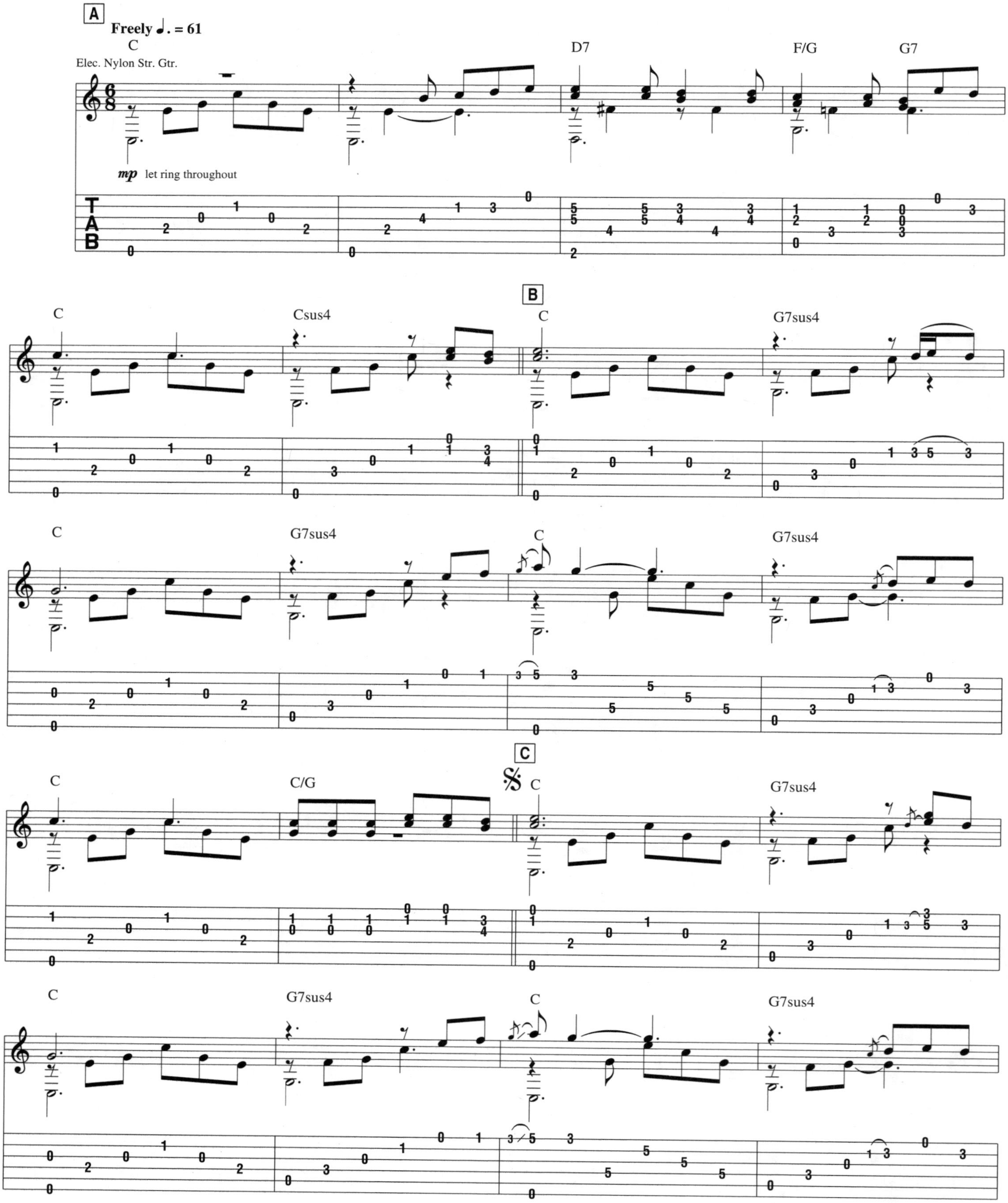

A

Freely ♩. = 61

C D7 F/G G7

Elec. Nylon Str. Gtr.

mp let ring throughout

C Csus4 **B** C G7sus4

C G7sus4 C G7sus4

C C/G **C** 𝄋 C G7sus4

C G7sus4 C G7sus4

To Coda 1
D
C
G7sus4
C
G7
C
G7/C
C
G7sus4
C
E
D7
F/G
G7
C
To Coda 2
D7
F/G
G7
Am/G
G
Em/G
G7
C
G7sus4
C
F
E♭
B♭7sus4
E♭

B♭7sus4
E♭
B♭7sus4
E♭
G
G7
D.S. al Coda 1
A Tempo
rit.
Coda 1
C
G7
C
G7/C
C
G7sus4
C
G7sus4
D.S.S. al Coda 2
Coda 2
G7
C
G7sus4
C
G7sus4
rit.
C

A Little Mark Musik

Written by Chet Atkins

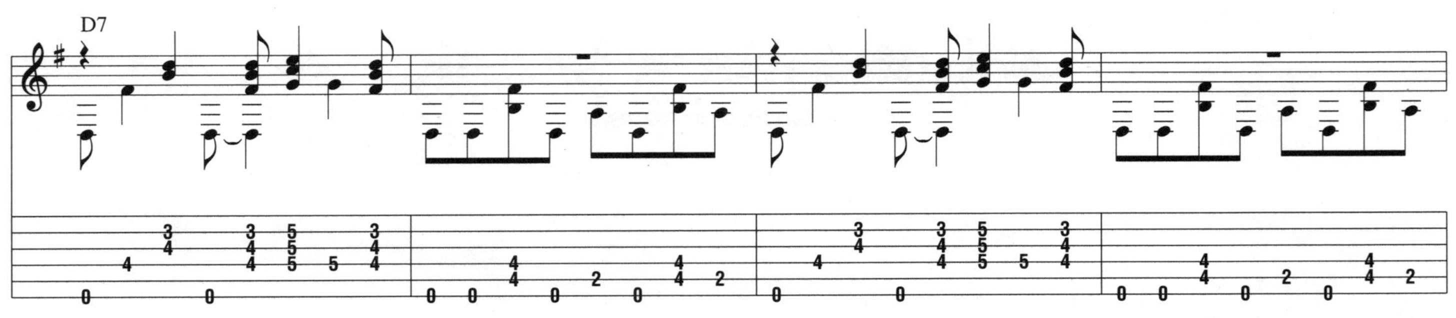
D7

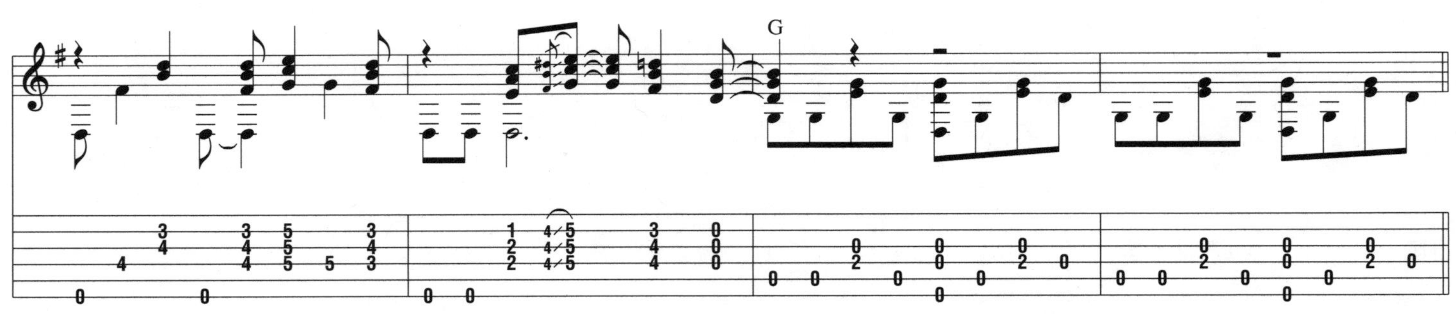
G

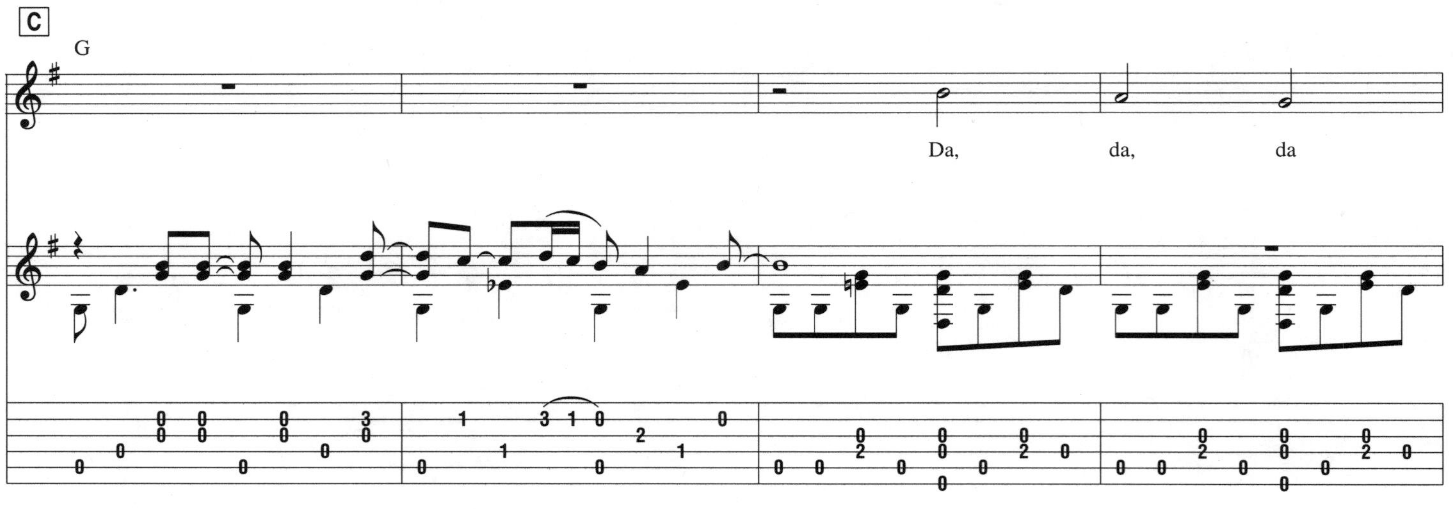
C
G
Da,
da,
da

da.
Da,
da,
da,

C
da.
Da,
da,
da,
D7
da.
G

D
G
C
G
D7

G
E
B♭
Csus2
B♭
A
B♭
Csus2
D7
m i p
let ring

G
F
G
Da, da, da,
G
da.
Da, da, da,
C
da.

G
Da,
da,
da,
D7
da.
G
D7
3

G
D7
G
moving barre
p i a i
m
moving barre
steady gliss.

Jam Man

Written by Chet Atkins

"Jam Man" utilizes a musical tool by that name on which it is possible to lay down a rhythm track and then layer other parts. I sometimes feature it on my shows, with the guitar doing all the music parts and my right hand overdubbing the percussion (kick drum and snare sounds). A Les Paul I'm Not! But it is fun to try.

G Am G F7 E Am
End Riff A
End Riff A1
let ring
C
w/ Rhy. Fig. 1 & Riffs A & *A1
Am G Am G C G7
Riff B
Riff B1
*w/ digital delay
* 1200 ms delay time. Delay is also used on Riff A1, next 11 meas.
C G#°7 Am G Am G F E
End Riff B
End Riff B1
D
w/ Riffs A & B, 1st 8 meas.
Am F D7/F# G9sus4 E7(#5)
*A.H.
A.H.
full
* To play artificial harmonics, fret string as shown in TAB, touch string 12 frets higher with tip of right-hand index-finger, and sound harmonic with thumb pick.

Am
G
Am
G
B♭9
A.H.
A.H.
A.H.
A.H.
A.H.
1/2
1/2
*P.M.
* down-stemmed notes only
A7(♯5)
D9
G7
E7(♯5)
1/2
1/2
Am
E
w/ Rhy. Fig. 1
Am
G
Am
w/ bar
-1/2

G C G C G#°7

Am G Am G F7

1/2

1/2

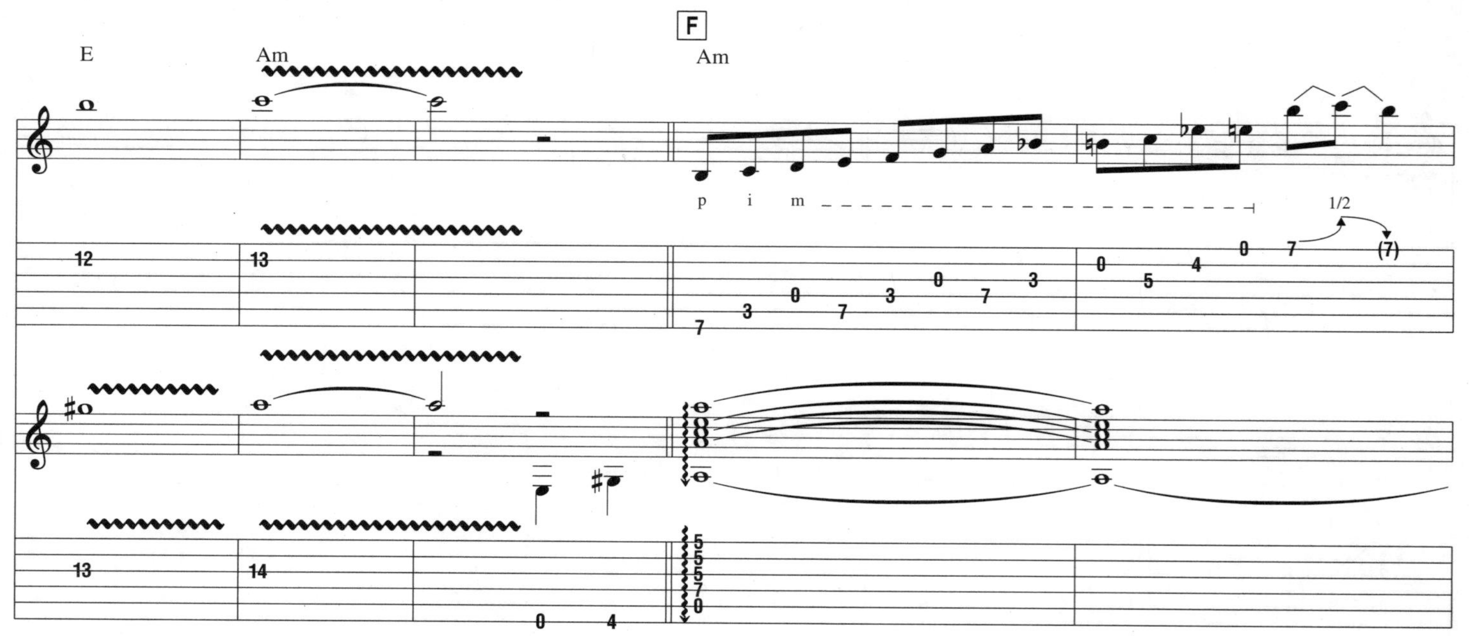

Am7
B°7
m i p
1/2
Am
Am7
F
E
Am
P.M.
let ring
P.M.

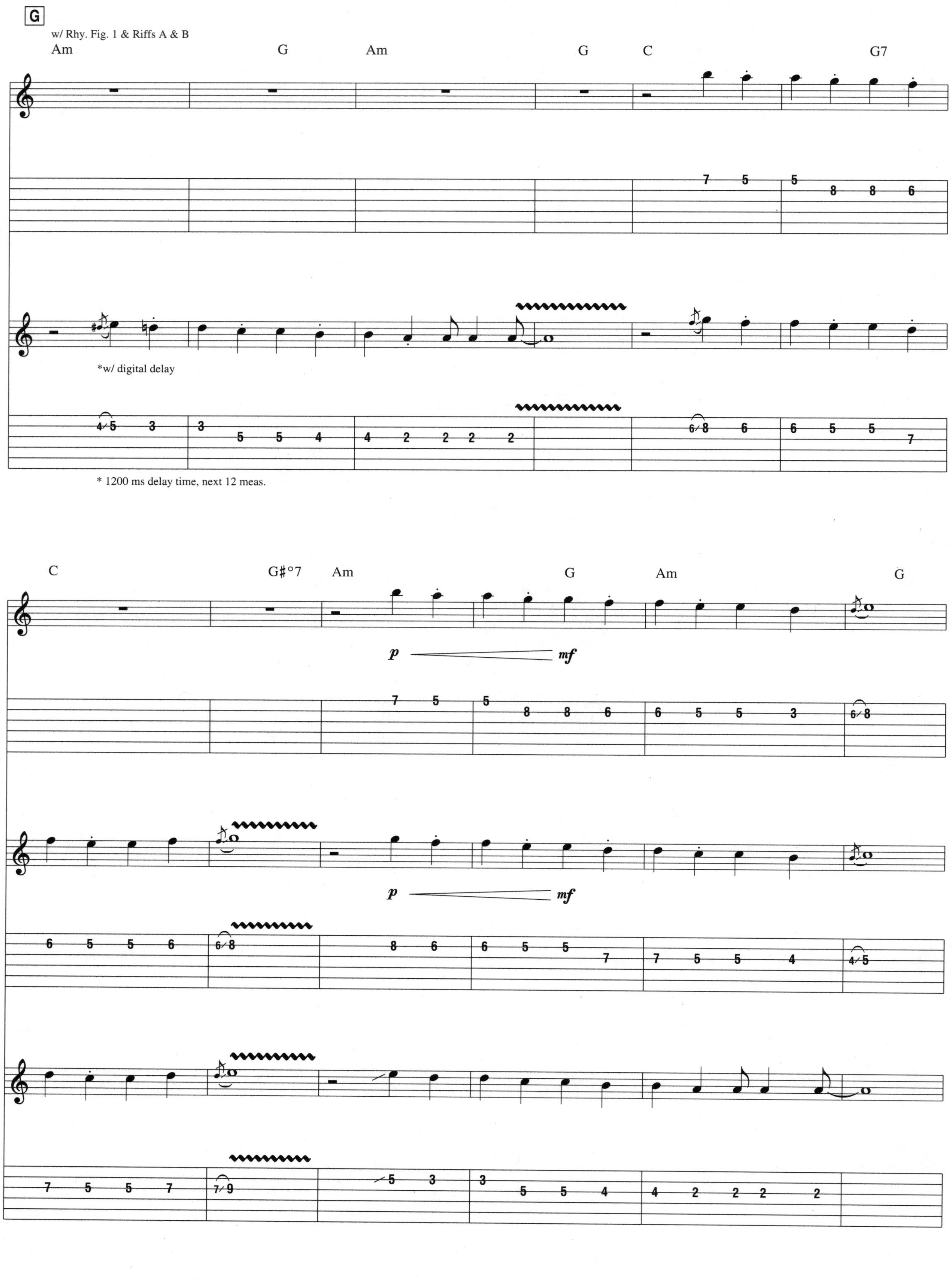

* 1200 ms delay time, next 12 meas.

C G♯°7 Am G Am G

p — *mf*

p — *mf*

F
E
Am
1/2
-1/2 w/ bar
-1/2
1/2

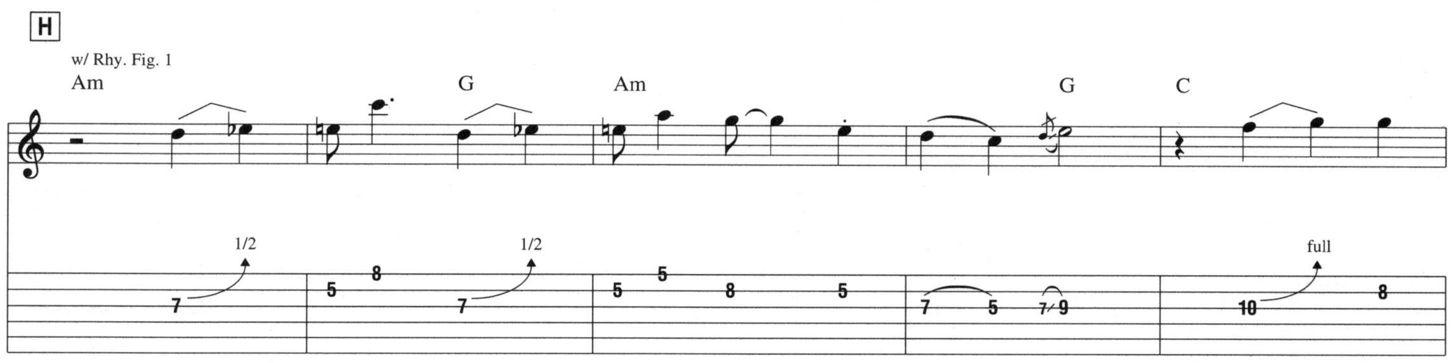
H
w/ Rhy. Fig. 1
Am
G
Am
G
C
1/2
1/2
full

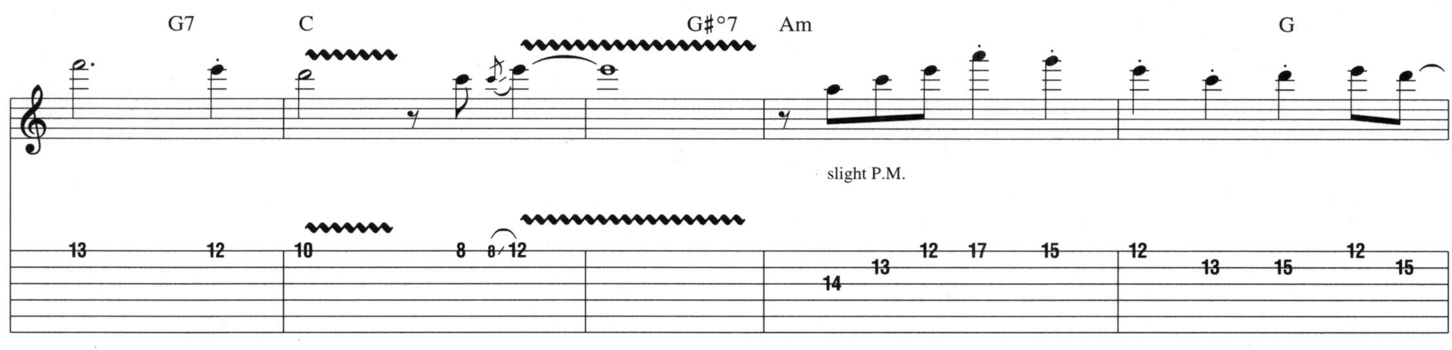
G7
C
G#°7
Am
G
slight P.M.

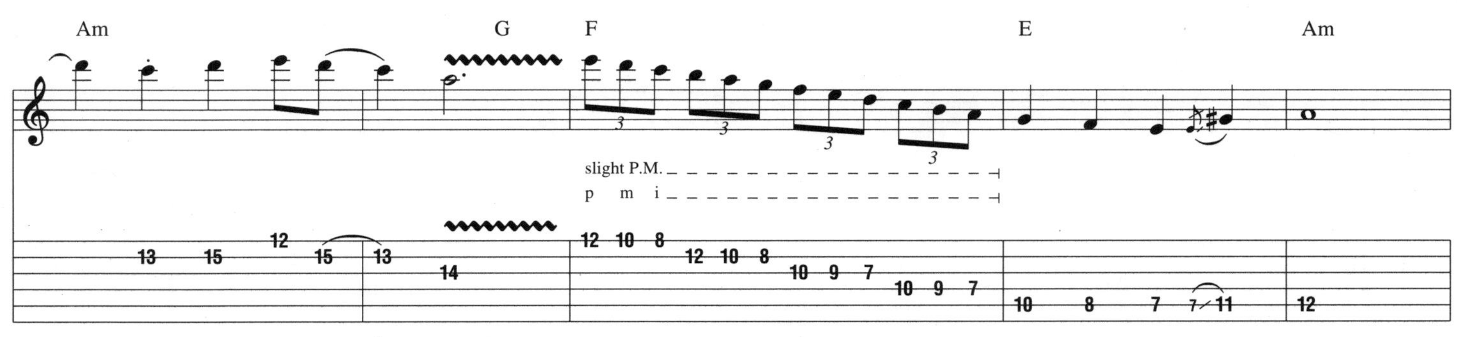
Am
G
F
E
Am
slight P.M.
p m i

I
w/ Rhy. Fig. 1, 1st 14 meas.
Am
G
Am
i p i m
G
C
G7
C
G#°7
i
full

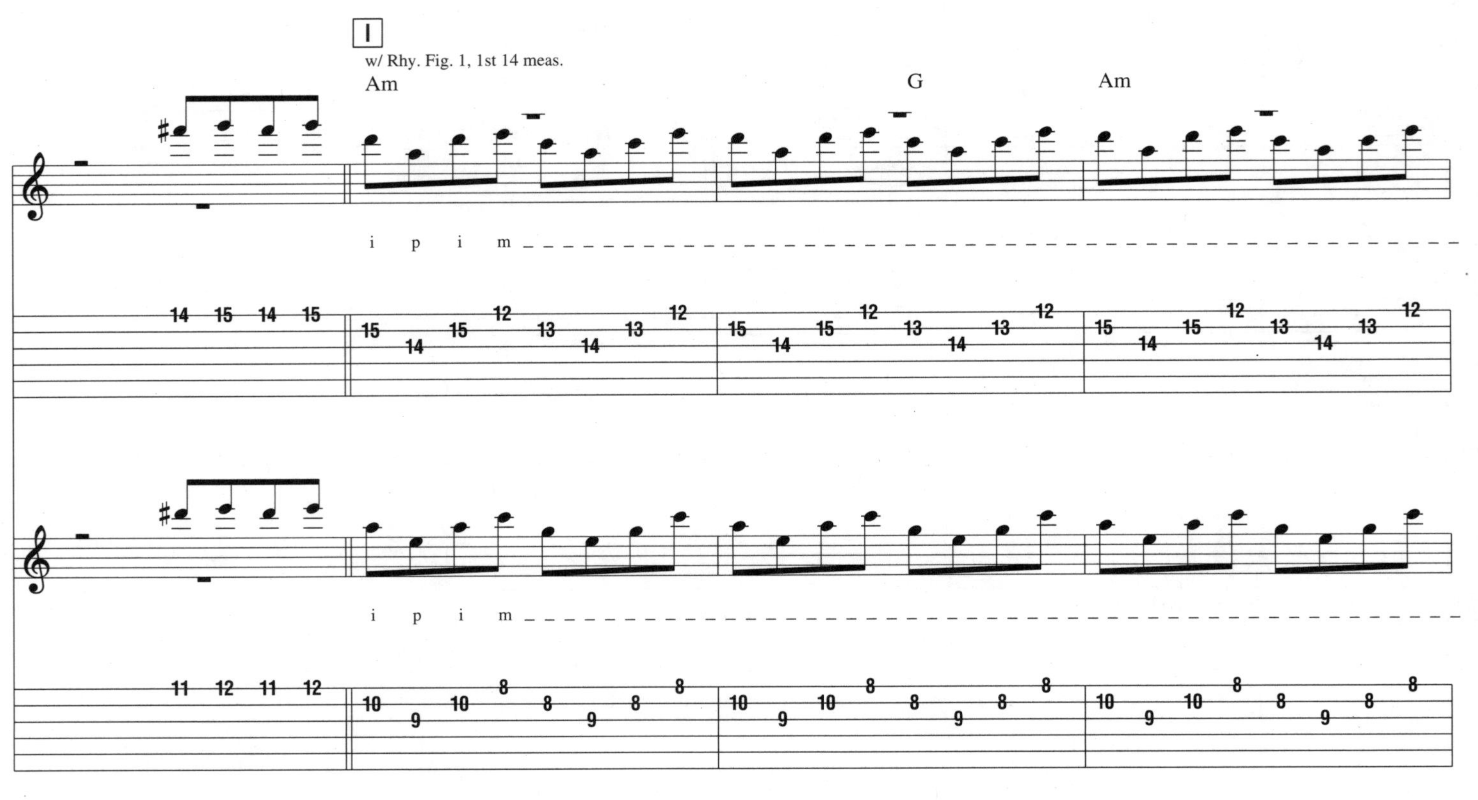

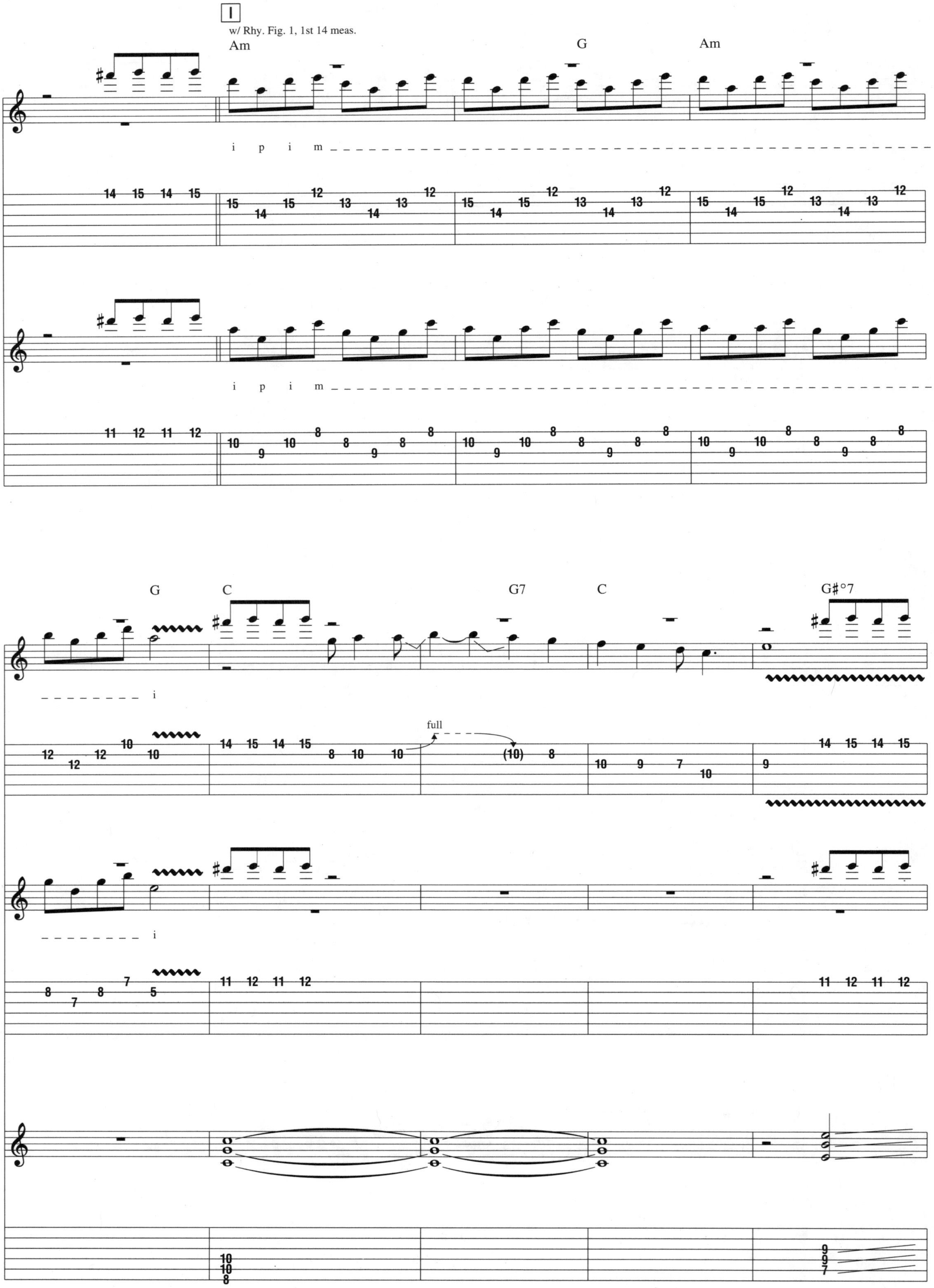

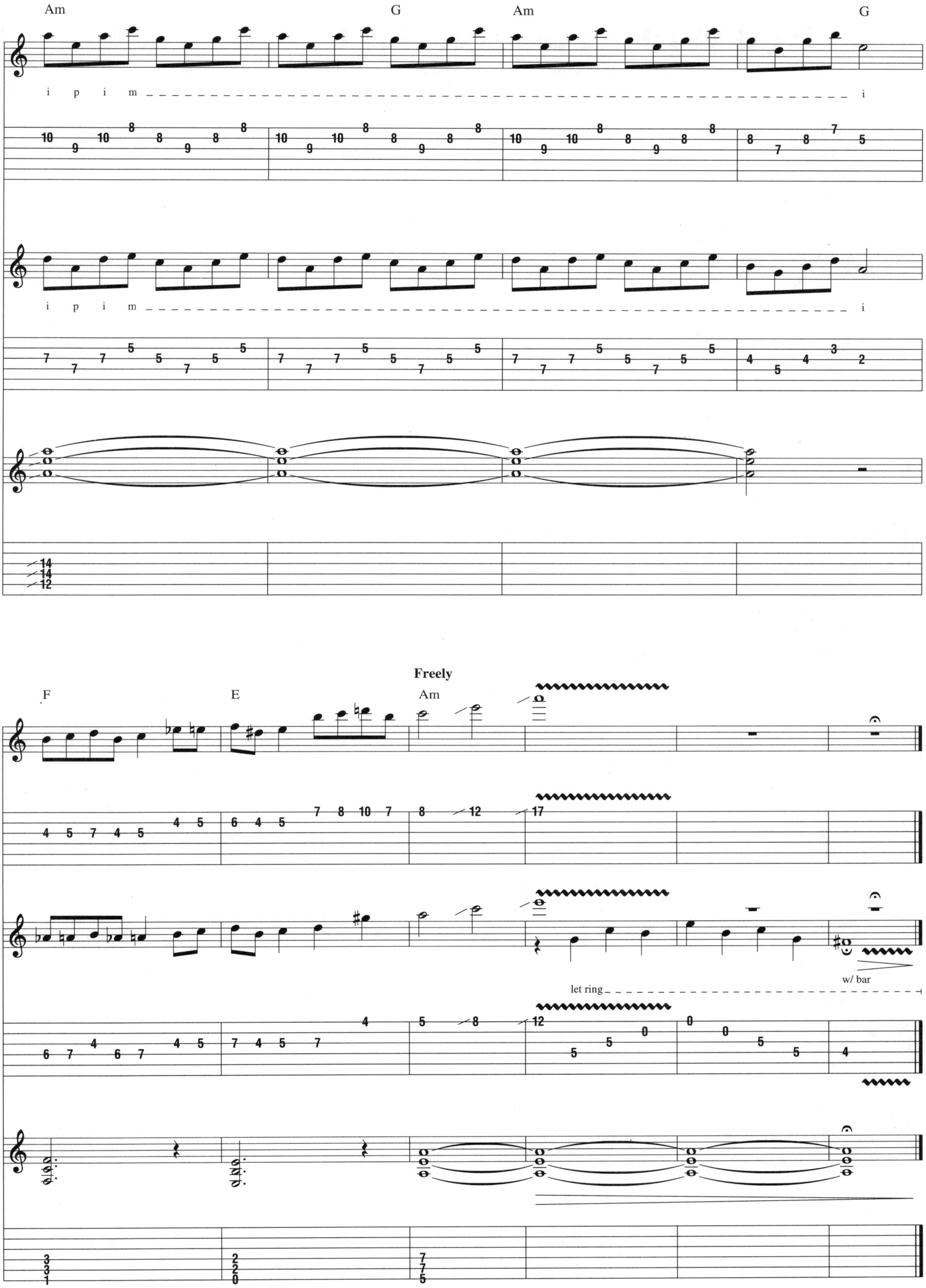

Am G Am G

i p i m i

i p i m i

Freely

F E Am

let ring

w/ bar

I Still Write Your Name in the Snow

Written by Chet Atkins and Billy Edd Wheeler

G
C
dar - lin' I think you'd like to know that I
G
D7
G
still write your name in the snow. Spoken: That's
C Bridge
C
G
right! When the snow - flakes fall, I guess I see
D7
G
A♭7/E♭
that hap - py you and me that used to be.

G9/D G7 C G B7/F#
And when the snow has cov - ered all ___ the ground _
Em7 A7 D9
I hear your name and have to write it down.
D Chorus
G C
Spoken: Yeah, Well, _ do you think _ of me when you're feel - in' low ____
G Em7 D7 G
and wish you could write my name ___ in the snow?

E Guitar Solo
C6
C#°7
G
G6
D13
D+9
D9
G13
C6
C#°7
G6
B7/F#
Em7
A7
D7
F Interlude
G13
(strings)
G9
G7
C7

A7
D7
N.C.(G)
A7
D7sus4
G
G Verse
G
2. Well I once had an
G7
C
G
ink - lin' that you'd come back a - gain.
I see now that

Em7
A7
D7
G7
I was just a - tink - lin' in the wind. You've hurt me
C7
G
more than you'll ev - er know and I still
D7
G
write your name in the snow. Spoken: Well,
H Bridge
C
G
when those snow - flakes fall I guess I see that

D7
G7
A♭9/E♭
G9/D
G7
hap - py you and me that used to be.
C
G
B7/F♯
Em7
I write your name so beau - ti - ful - ly but it's
A7
D9
D7
hard to cross the i's and dot the t's.
I Chorus
G
C7
Do you think of me when you're feel - in' low and

G
D7
G
E7
wish you could write my name ___ in the snow?
J Outro
A9
D9
G
E7
Spoken: Now, the beautiful Bluegrass ending that you can sing in
A9
D9
G
E7
three-part harmony like this:
Son-of-a-gun, I'm
A7
D9
G
tired of liv-in' this way, hot-a-might-y damn.

Pu, Uana Hulu
(Remembering Gabby)
By David Alapai

C
G7
C
N.C.
D
C
C7
Fmaj7
G7
C
C7
Fmaj7

G7
C
E
G7
C
N.C.
F
F
G7
C
* even
Fmaj7/C
G7
C/G
* Played as even eighth notes.
G
C
F/A
C7/G
F

* To play artificial harmonic, fret string as shown in TAB, touch string 12 frets higher with tip of right-hand index-finger, and sound harmonic with thumb pick.

Happy Again

Written by Chet Atkins

1.
E7
E+9
let ring
2.
E7
Aadd9
N.C.
C Bridge
Dmaj7
1/2 VII
A+9/D
1/2 VI
let ring
1/2 VI
V
Dmaj7
E7
A
E7
A
C#7/G#
G9
F#m7
II
II
Bm9
Cadd9
E7/B
E+9

D Theme
A
Amaj7
Eadd9
A6
A
G9♭5
D/F♯
E7
Aadd9
N.C.
let ring
E Bridge
Dmaj7
1/2 VII
A+9/D
1/2 VI
Dmaj7
V
V
E7
A
E7
A

C#7/G#
G9
F#m7
II
Bm9
E
p m i
p
F
Theme
A
Amaj7
A6
A
G9add#4

D/F♯
E7
Aadd9
let ring
Aadd9/B
E7
let ring
let ring
G Outro
Aadd9
let ring
Bm7
E7sus4
let ring
let ring
rit.
let ring
A

Sweet Alla Lee

Written by Chet Atkins

G9
C
A7
E
D7
G7
C
F
G7
C
F
C
p a m i
F
G7
G
C
G7
C

F
G7
C
H
F
C
A7
D7
G7
C
F
G7
F♯m7♭5
B7
I
E7
A

B7
E
J
E7
A
B7
E7
K
A
E
E
D7
C#9
F#7
B7
L
E7
A6

B7
E
G7
M
C
F
G7
C
G
N
C
F
F/G
C
C9
O
F
C

P
A7
D7
G
C
F
F/G
C
Q
C
F
G7
C
R
C
F
G7

S
C
F
C
A7
D7
G7
T
C
E7/B
Am
C/G
F
A7
Dm
D♯°7
C/E
C
D7/A
G7/B
C
D7/F♯
G7sus4
C
N.C.

Maybelle

Written by Chet Atkins

Gtr. 1: Capo VII

*Paul Yandell ** Symbols in parentheses represent chord names respective to capoed guitar. Symbols above reflect actual sounding chord. Capoed fret is "0" in TAB.

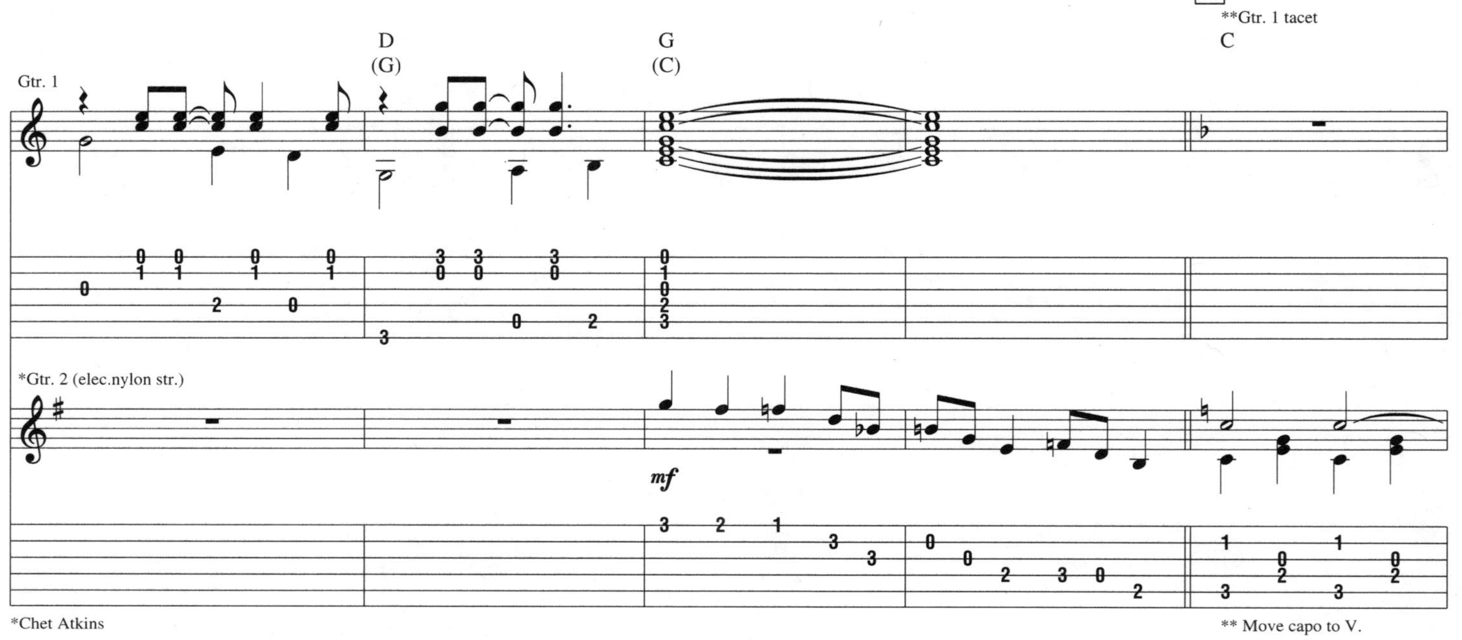

*Chet Atkins

** Move capo to V.

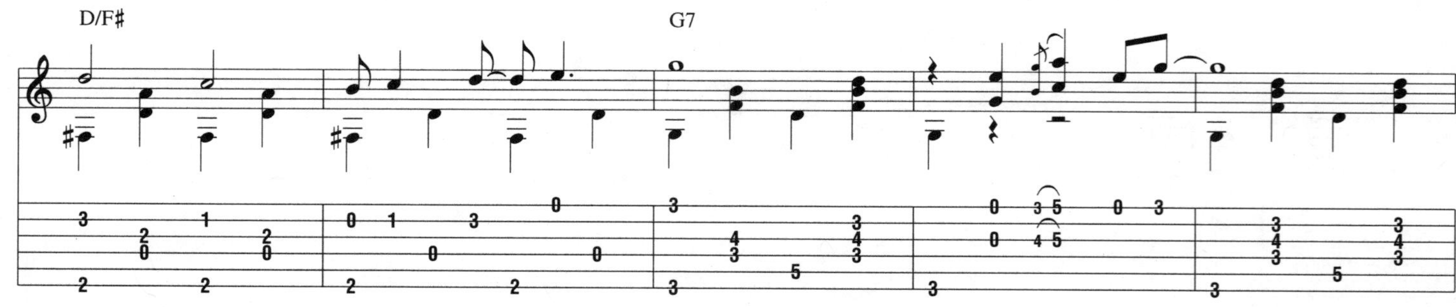

G7 N.C.
(D7)
Riff A
C
C
(G)
End Riff A
Rhy. Fig. 1
Gtr. 1
w/ pick
slight P.M.
Gtr. 2
p i m
* muted
E7
(B7)
F
(C)
slight P.M.
D/F♯
(A/C♯)
G7
(D7)
slight P.M.

N.C.
C
(G)
End Rhy. Fig. 1
slight P.M.
* muted
D
G7
(D7)
Rhy. Fig. 2
End Rhy. Fig. 2
slight P.M.
Gtr. 1: w/ Rhy. Fig. 2, 2 times
Gtr. 2

Gtr. 1: w/ Riff A
N.C.
* muted
E
Gtr. 1: w/ Rhy. Fig. 1
C
(G)
E7
(B7)
F
(C)
D9
(A9)
G7
(D7)
N.C.
C
(G)

F
C
(G)
Gtr. 1
Rhy. Fig. 3
G7
(D7)
slight P.M.
Gtr. 2
sim.
End Rhy. Fig. 3
Gtr. 1: w/ Rhy. Fig. 3
* sul pont.
* pluck near bridge next 7 meas.

G
Gtr. 1: w/ Rhy. Fig. 2, 3 times
C
(G)
G7
(D7)
Gtr. 1: w/ Riff A
N.C.
* muted
H
Gtr. 1: w/ Rhy. Fig. 1
C
(G)
E7
(B7)
F
(C)

D9
(A9)
G7
(D7)
N.C.
C
(G)
* muted
I
C
(G)
G7
(D7)
C
(G)
Gtr. 1
Rhy. Fig. 4
End Rhy. Fig. 4
slight P.M.
Gtr. 2
* sul pont.
* next 14 meas.
Gtr. 1: w/Rhy. Fig. 4
Gtr. 2
G7
(D7)
C
(G)

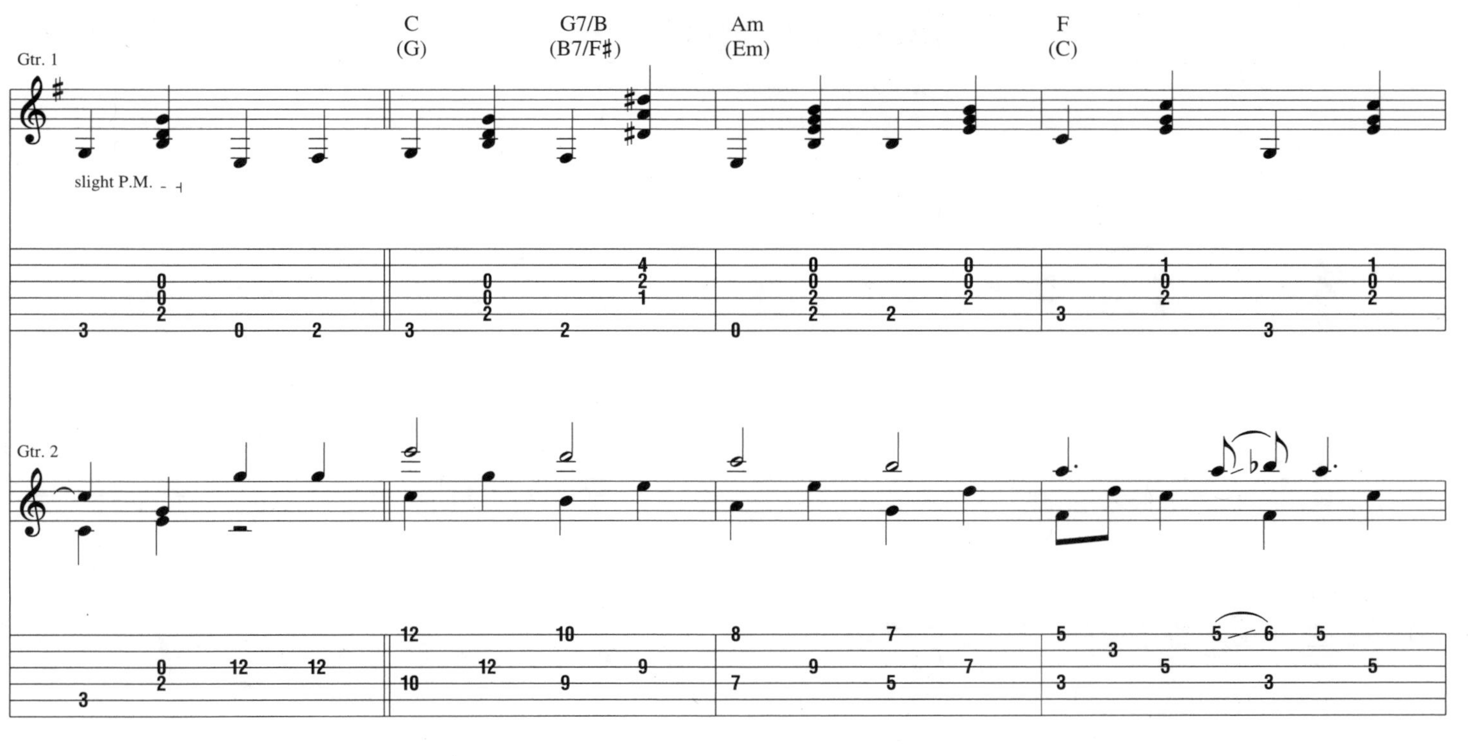

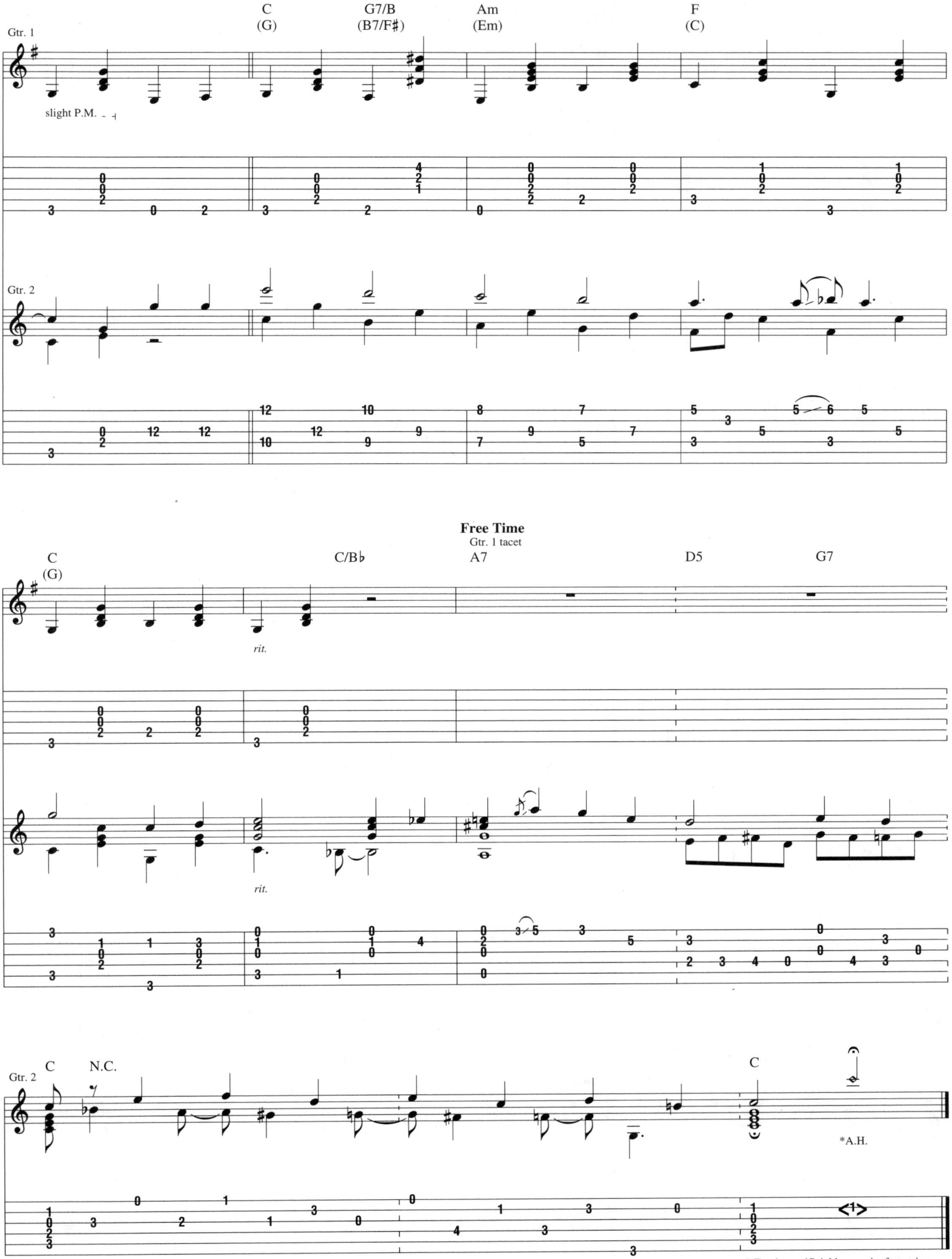

Gtr. 1
C (G)
G7/B (B7/F♯)
Am (Em)
F (C)
slight P.M.
Gtr. 2
C (G)
C/B♭
rit.
Free Time
Gtr. 1 tacet
A7
D5
G7
rit.
Gtr. 2
C
N.C.
C
*A.H.

* To play artificial harmonic, fret string as shown in TAB, touch string 12 frets higher with tip of right-hand index-finger, and sound harmonic with thumb pick.

Mr. Bojangles

Words and Music by Jerry Jeff Walker

C/G
D7/F♯
D7
E7
F13
CI
i p m i p m
* muted
F♯+7
II
G7
III
D Verse
C
C/B
C/A
C/G
F
F6
1/2 III
G7
III
N.C.
C
C/B
C/A
F
F6
1/2 III
G7
III
E
Fmaj7
VII
Em7
VII
E7
Am
1/2 V

C/G
D7/F#
D7
B♭9
A9
A♭9
F Chorus
G6
Am9
G7
III
N.C.(G7)
Am9
G7
III
N.C.(G7)
Am9
G7
III
III
G
C
C/B
C/A
H Verse
N.C.(G7)
C
C/B
Am
C/G
F

I
G9
C
C/B
Am
1/2 V
C/G
F
I
G9
I
Fmaj7
VIII
Em7
VII
E7
Am
C/G
D/F#
D7
G7
Am7
i p m i p m
A#°7
G7/B
J Verse
C6
X
B°7sus4
IX
A7sus4
p m i p m i

C/G
V
F7♯11
F7
Gadd9sus4/D
G7
III
p m i p m
C6
X
B°7sus4
IX
A7sus4
C/G
V
F7♯11
p m i p m i
F7
Gadd9sus4/D
G7
III
p m i p m
K
Fmaj7
VIII
VII
Em7
VII
E7
Am
C/G
D/F♯
D7
B♭9
1/2 III
A9
1/2 II
A♭9
1/2 I
G9

L Chorus
Am9
G7
N.C.(G7)
Am9
G7
1/2 III
N.C.(G7)
Am9
G7
M
C
C/B
C/A
N.C.(G7)
N Outro
C
C/B
B♭
F/A
A♭9
rit.
G7
C
N.C.
D♭9/A♭
VI
Cadd9
V
p m i
p

Cheek to Cheek

Words and Music by Irving Berlin

G9♭5
F♯7
Bm7
F13
E7
C
G7add9
A
A♯°7
E7
A
A♯°7
E7
A
A♯°7
E7
A
F♯7
Bm7
E7
A
A♯°7
E7
A
A♯°7
E7
A
A♯°7
E7
A
F♯7

D
Bm7
E7
A
Am
Am/G♯
Am/G
Am/F♯
F7
Bm7
Am7add4
G♯m7
C♯7
F♯m7
B9
E13
E7
E
Amaj7
A♯°7
E7
Amaj7
A♯°7
E7
Amaj7
Bm7
B♯°7
Aadd9/C♯
C♯7♯9
F♯7
B7
E7
G9♭5
F♯7
Bm7
F13
E7
G9♭5

F
A A#°7 E7 A A#°7 E7 A A#°7
E7 A F#7 Bm7 E7 A A#°7 E7
A A#°7 E7 A Bm E7 A F#7
G
Bm7 E7 A Am Am/G# Am/G Am/F# F13
F7 Bm9 E(no 3rd) Bm/G# C#7 F#m7 B9 E7

H
Amaj7 F#7 B7 E7 Amaj7 F#7 B7 E7 Amaj7 Bm7
rit.
B#°7 Aadd9/C# C#7 C#+7 F#9 B7
rit.
I
Freely
E9 E F9 E9
i p i m
C#m Cm Bm G9♭5 F#7
A Tempo
Bm7 F13
E7 C#m7 F#+7 F#7 Bm9 E9
N.C.(A7) (A) B/A A

You Do Something to Me

Words and Music by Cole Porter

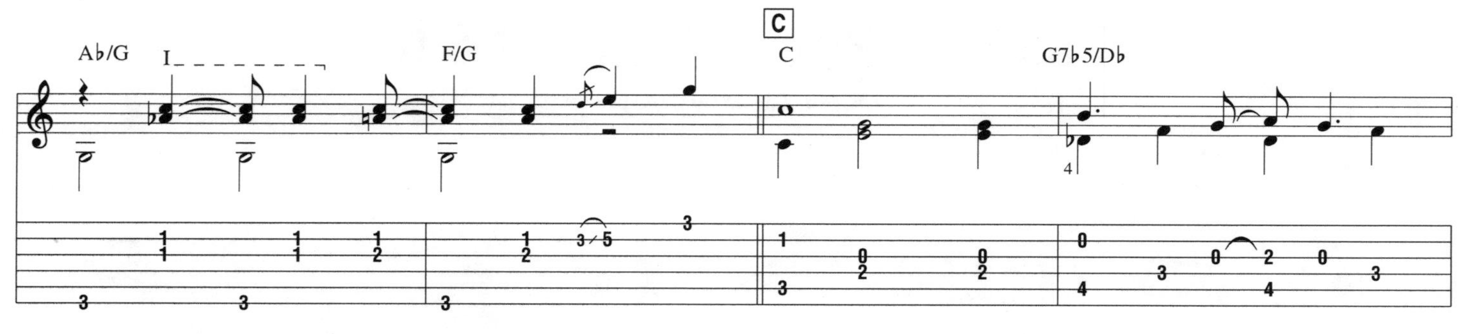
C
A♭/G
I
F/G
C
G7♭5/D♭

C
F7
Em
Am7
A7/C♯

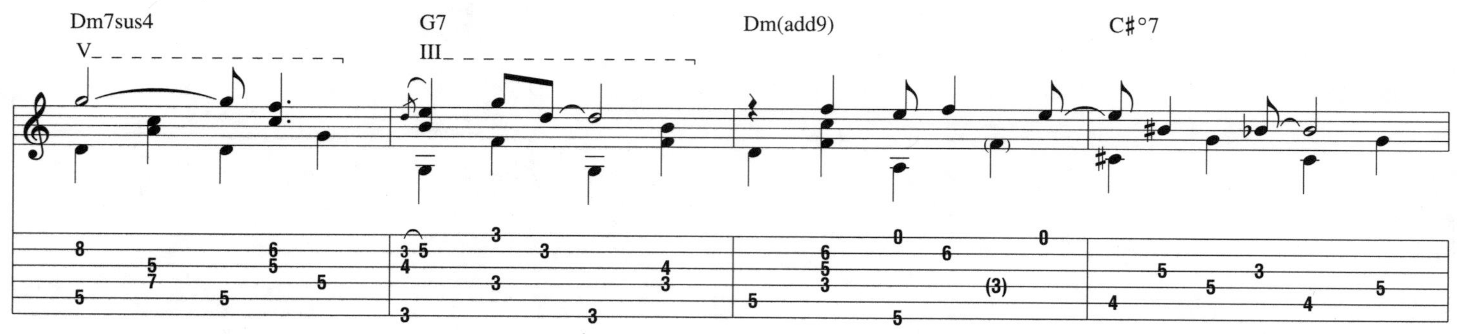
Dm7sus4
V
G7
III
Dm(add9)
C♯°7

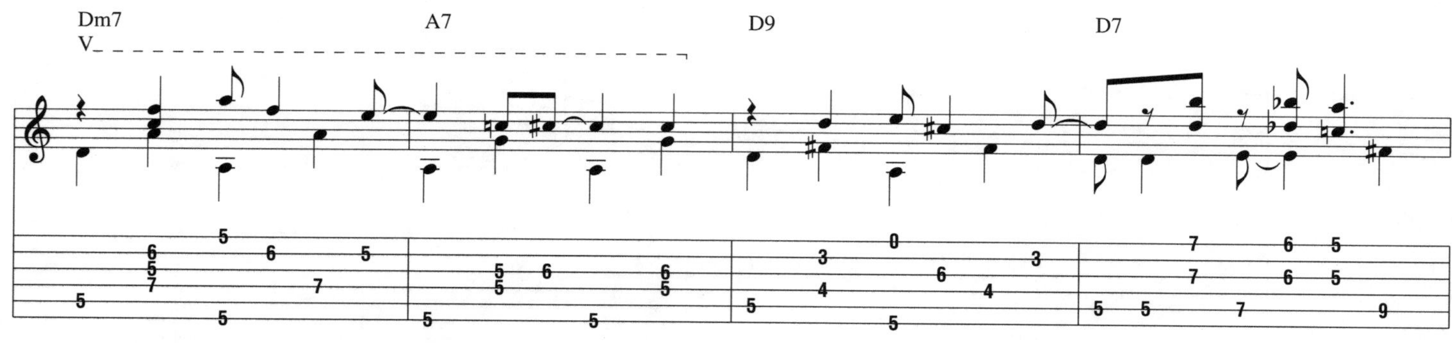
Dm7
V
A7
D9
D7

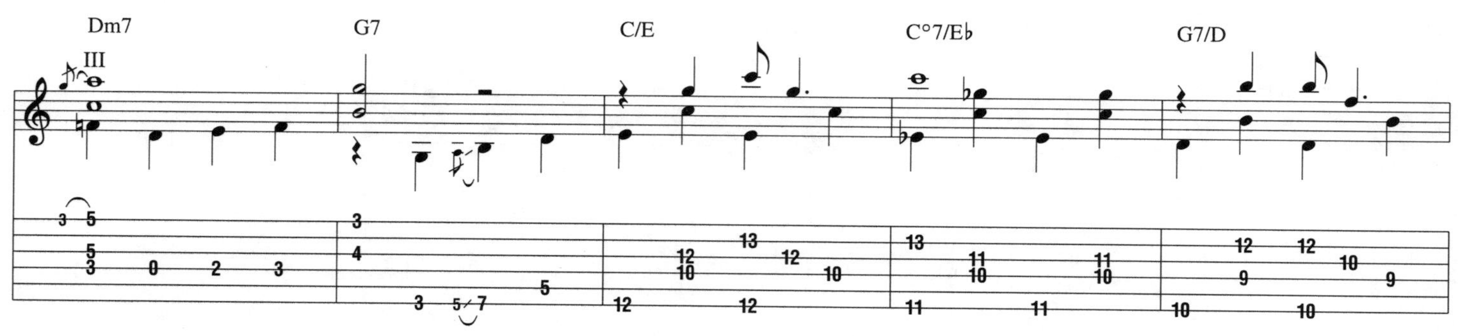
Dm7
III
G7
C/E
C°7/E♭
G7/D

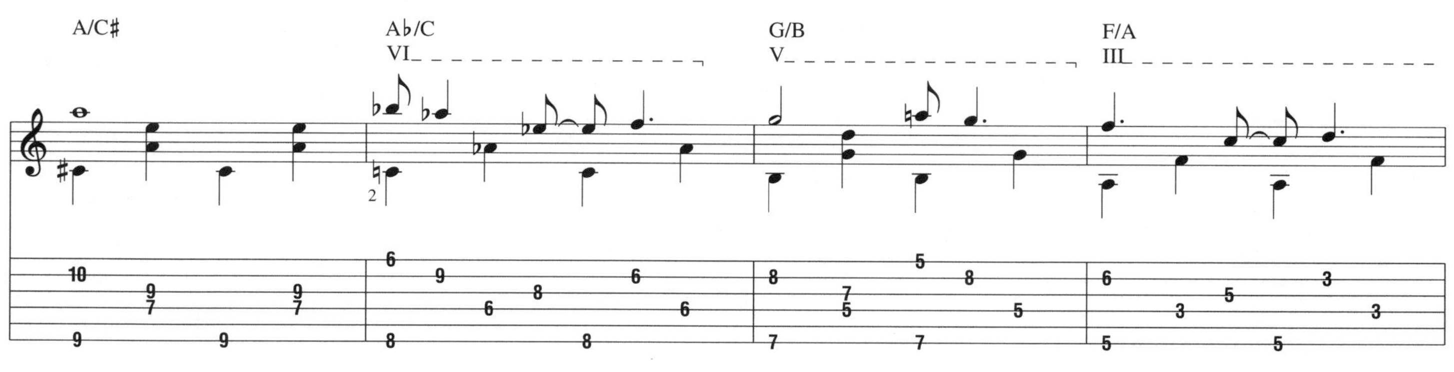

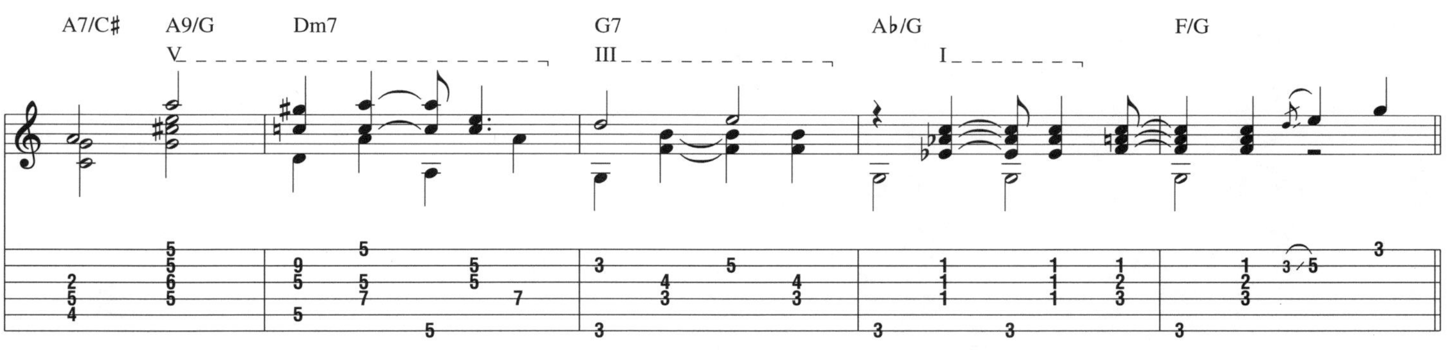

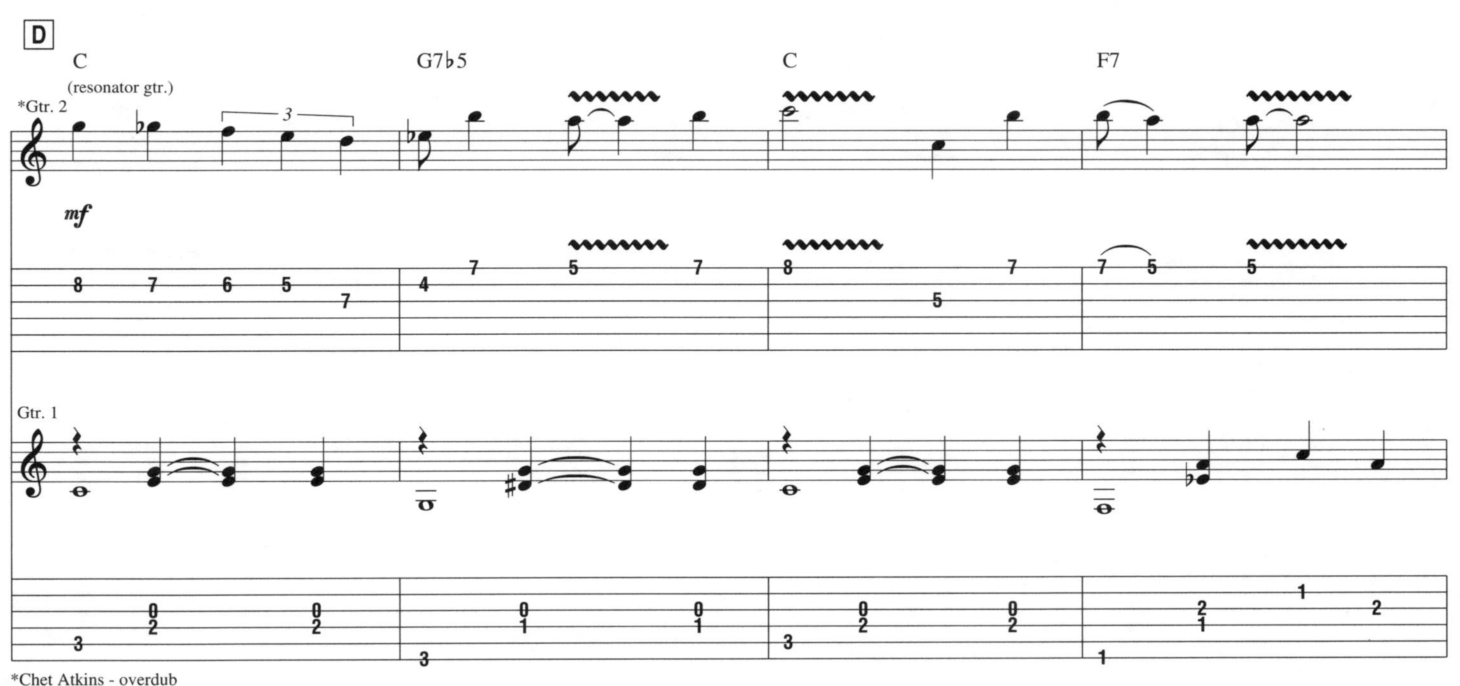

*Chet Atkins - overdub

Em
Am7
A7/C♯
Dm7
G7
1/2
1/2
Dm7
C♯°7
Dm7
A7/C♯
A
D
E♭9/B♭
D9
Dm7
G13

C
B7
B♭7
A7
VIII
VII
VI
V
A♭7
G7
F
G13
Gtr. 2 tacet
C
B+7
C
E7
A7
VIII
VII

Dm9
G13
D7/A
G7
V
III
Gtr. 2 tacet
Dm7
G7
C
G7♭5/D♭
Gtr. 1
V
III
Gtr. 1 C
E7
A7
Dm7
G7
V
Gtr. 2
Gtr. 2 tacet
A♭/G
F/G
C13
Gtr. 1
gliss.
gliss.

Ave Maria

Arranged by Chet Atkins

C
G
B/G
1/2IV
Em
F#7
IV
1/2 II
F#°7
IV
Em
A7
1/2 V
D
E7/B
D/A
II
A
1/2 II
D
D7
D
D7
G
D7
Em
D
B
IV
Am
VII
V

Cmaj7
V
A7
II
C♯°7
D7
E
G
Em
G/D
D7
G
G7
C/G
Cm/G
G
F
G
Em
G/D
D7
G
G7
G°7
Cm/G
G
G
Harm.

More Fingerstyle Favorites

from HAL•LEONARD®

12 Wedding Songs

arranged for medium voice and fingerstyle guitar

The collection combines classical/traditional and popular selections. The guitar part is presented in both standard notation and tablature. Contents: Annie's Song • Ave Maria (Shubert) • The First Time I Saw Your Face • Here, There And Everywhere • I Swear • If • In My Life • Jesu, Joy Of Man's Desiring • Let It Be Me • Unchained Melody • When I Fall In Love • You Needed Me.

00740007 .... $12.95

American Folk Songs For Fingerstyle Guitar

25 songs, including: Amazing Grace • America The Beautiful • Home On The Range • I've Been Working On The Railroad • My Old Kentucky Home • When Johnny Comes Marching Home • and more.

00698981 .... $12.95

Broadway Ballads for Guitar

24 arrangements, including: All I Ask Of You • Bewitched • I Dreamed A Dream • Memory • My Funny Valentine • What I Did For Love • and more.

00698984 .... $10.95

Classic Blues for Voice and Fingerstyle Guitar

20 arrangements with guitar accompaniment and solos, including: Mercury Blues • Seventh Son • Little Red Rooster • Trouble In Mind • Nobody Knows You When You're Down And Out • and more.

00698992 .... $12.95

Contemporary Movie Songs For Solo Guitar

24 arrangements of silver screen gems, including: Endless Love • The John Dunbar Theme ("Dances With Wolves") • Theme From "Ordinary People" • Somewhere Out There • Unchained Melody • and more. Includes notes and tab.

00698982 .... $14.95

Disney Fingerstyle Guitar

14 fun favorites, including: Under The Sea • Beauty And The Beast • A Whole New World • Can You Feel The Love Tonight • and more.

00690009 .... $12.95

Gospel Favorites For Fingerstyle Guitar

25 classics, including: Amazing Grace • Because He Lives • El Shaddai • How Great Thou Art • The Old Rugged Cross • Rock Of Ages • Will The Cradle Be Unbroken • Wings Of A Dove • and more. Includes notes and tab.

00698991 .... $12.95

International Favorites

25 songs that span the globe, including: Au Clair de la Lune • The Blue Bells Of Scotland • La Cucaracha • Londonderry Air • Santa Lucia • and more.

00698996 .... $12.95

Mannheim Steamroller – Christmas For Fingerstyle Guitar

Enjoy these world-famous Christmas arrangements from the best-selling Mannheim Steamroller albums. 10 pieces, including: Carol Of The Birds • The Holly And The Ivy • I Saw Three Ships • Wassail, Wassail • and more. Includes notes and tab.

00650042 .... $12.95

Fingerpicking Beatles

20 favorites, including: And I Love Her • Eleanor Rigby • Here Comes The Sun •Here, There And Everywhere • Hey Jude • Michelle • Norwegian Wood • While My Guitar Gently Weeps • Yesterday • and more.

00699404 .... $14.95

Eric Clapton Fingerstyle Guitar Collection

12 Clapton classics for fingerstyle guitar. Includes: Bell Bottom Blues • Cocaine • Layla • Nobody Knows You When You're Down And Out • Strange Brew • Tears In Heaven • Wonderful Tonight • and 5 more favorites.

00699411 .... $10.95

A Fingerstyle Guitar Christmas

29 great fingerstyle arrangements, including: Angels We Have Heard On High • Auld Lang Syne • The First Noel • Good King Wenceslas • The Holly And The Ivy • Jingle Bells • O Little Town Of Bethlehem • Up On The Housetop • What Child Is This? • and more.

00699038 .... $12.95

Billy Joel – The Fingerstyle Collection

15 of his most popular hits arranged for fingerstyle guitar, including: Honesty • Just The Way You Are • My Life • Piano Man • Uptown Girl • and more.

00699410 .... $12.95

Elton John – The Fingerstyle Collection

15 fingerstyle arrangements, including: Your Song • Daniel • Bennie And The Jets • Crocodile Rock • Don't Go Breaking My Heart • Candle In The Wind • and more. Includes notes and tab.

00699414 .... $14.95

TV Tunes For Guitar

23 fingerstyle arrangements of America's most memorable TV themes, including: The Addams Family • The Brady Bunch • Coach • Frasier • Happy Days • Hill Street Blues • I Love Lucy • Mister Ed • Northern Exposure • The Odd Couple • St. Elsewhere • and more.

00698985 .... $12.95

For More Information, See Your Local Music Dealer, Or Write To:

7777 W. Bluemound Rd. P.O. Box 13819 Milwaukee, WI 53213
HTTP://WWW.HALLEONARD.COM

Prices, contents, and availability subject to change without notice. Some products may not be available outside the U.S.A.